INTRODUCTION

Buxton, one of the highest towns in England, is a good centre for touring Derbyshire's Peak District. Famous for its spa and sheltered by surrounding hills, the town was familiar to the Romans and Mary Queen of Scots and was developed by the 5th Duke of Devonshire. Some of the most interesting country surrounds Buxton, not least of which is Axe Edge Moor. Here, some of Derbyshire's most beautiful rivers such as the Wye and Dove rise on superb moorland which is fine walking country with splendid views. The River Dove, rich in trout, flows south through Dove Dale, the most beautiful of Derbyshire's dales. It makes its way swiftly through a wooded limestone gorge of caves and crags and forms a natural boundary with Staffordshire. Ashbourne at the foot of the Peak District is an at Sl pl is part of the country.

North east of here are the Matlocks, an area of towns and villages surrounded by woodland and limestone cliffs. Stone circles, Norman churches and some very fine old houses offer historians and archaeologists a feast. The caves around here were originally lead mines, worked by the Romans. The River Derwent flows through this part of the district. Walks may be taken through wooded countryside and the scenery is very pleasant indeed. This is an area of hills and beautiful river valleys and has a wealth of history to offer the visitor.

CONTENTS

UNDERSTANDING THE MAP	4
PATHS AND OLD ROADS	5
TOWNS AND VILLAGES	10
PLACE NAMES	13
CANALS AND RIVERS	15
CASTLES, CHURCHES AND HALLS	17
RAILWAYS	22
ANCIENT SITES	27
NATURE	29
INDUSTRIAL ARCHAEOLOGY	31
TOURIST INFORMATION	34

A cottage with flower-filled garden at Ilam (Ref: 1350. Picture: D. Pratt)
River Wye at Monsal Dale (Ref: 1871. Picture: D. Pratt)

© Alan Kind 1990. All rights reserved. No part of this publication may be reproduced without the prior permission of David & Charles plc. Typeset by Typesetters (Birmingham) Ltd, Smethwick, West Midlands and printed in Great Britain by Redwood Press Ltd, Melksham, Wiltshire for David & Charles plc   Brunel House   Newton Abbot   Devon

UNDERSTANDING THE MAP

Any spot on a Landranger 1/50,000 map can be located by use of a National Grid reference. This is done by noting which vertical line falls to the left of the location and then which horizontal line falls below the location. For example, if we had arranged to meet a friend at the Youth hostel near Ilam this falls within the one kilometre square labelled 130500.

We next estimate tenths of a square to the right of the vertical grid line, and tenths of a square above the horizontal grid line, to give a standard six figure grid reference which, in this case, is 131506. You may find it helpful to imagine nine vertical lines and nine horizontal lines in each small square when doing this. On the ground these imaginary lines represent squares of one hundred metres edge (about a hundred and ten old fashioned yards).

Some important guide books, such as those of the National Trust and the Ramblers Association, now use map references and from these the exact location of anything from a stately home to a farmhouse offering bed and breakfast can be identified.

Here is another example. If we wish to refer to Stoop Farm in Dove Dale in kilometre square 060680 then, by estimating tenths of a square, we get the full six-figure reference 063681.

This is all that is needed by way of referencing on a single Landranger map although, by adding letters to a reference, one can specify anywhere in Britain, on any modern Ordnance Survey (OS) map, of any scale. If you are interested in doing this, look at the instructions in the margin of the map.

Here is a useful hint for reading and measuring OS map references: "across the plain and up the hill". This will remind you to run your eye horizontally from left to right to get the "Eastings" before you run your eye from bottom to top to get the "Northings". Remember that the hints tell you which way you must run your eyes NOT which way the grid lines run!

Right, what is the six figure OS reference for the church at Morley which is in the bottom right hand corner of the map? Next what feature is located by 276655? If you get these two OS references right you can get any OS references right.

(Answers: The church at Morley is at 396409. The OS reference 276655 gives the site of the triangulation pillar near Bumper Castle).

Reading a map reference

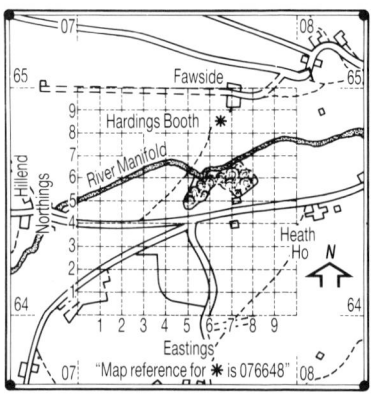

PATHS AND OLD ROADS

This area has been described as, 'not over-powering with history but filled with Nature's lovely places, packed with natural beauty in infinite variety, from magnificent Peakland heights to caverns deep in the heart of rock'. This is a truly apt description of an area offering something to the serious walker and Sunday afternoon explorer alike.

Seventeenth and eighteenth century travellers would have found that the Peak District contained some of the wildest terrain in all England, but evidence shows that large parts of Derbyshire were settled even before the arrival of the Romans. What follows will be a description of the development of pathways and roads from the Roman period to the present day.

Roman roads – A well-marked alignment of a Roman road runs north westward over the high ground between Derby and Buxton, continuing on to Whaley Bridge and Manchester. The section of the road in this area is best joined on the east bank of the Derwent at Milford (347451). The route then continues past Belper by the Chevin Road which climbs Chevinside from a level of 200ft near the river to over 800ft on the high ground that is crossed on the way to Wirksworth (288540). A very direct road then leads on to Brassington (232547) keeping on high ground after the initial climbing. The road then runs north-west to the east of the High Peak Trail (211574), passing a little to the east of Minninglow. For half a mile to Pikehall (193592) a lane runs along the route, which then passes a tumulus (176613) on the crossing of the Middleton to Newhaven road, and another at Benty Grange (149642). The route then follows the A515 to the point where the road bears westerly towards Great Low. It then crosses Sterndale Moor where it rejoins the A515 again, half a mile to the south-east of Brierlow Bar (096693). The A515 then follows the route of the Roman road into Buxton itself where there was a Roman settlement, *Aquae*, valued for its medicinal waters. This is a convenient place to rest before continuing the route towards Whaley Bridge and on to Manchester.

Another Roman road led south-westward from Buxton to Leek (see Landranger number 118), and probably continued on to Stoke-on-Trent. On leaving Buxton (041721) the road has to adapt its route to climb along the eastern slopes of Axe Edge. It then follows ridges from Oliver Hill (030677) to Morridge Top (032653). The route is then straight to Leek, following the A53 except for a local deviation at the steep descent into Upper Hulme (015610). In fact, the road follows the route of the A53 continuously, apart from the sharp bend by Oliver Hill (031682), where the older and more direct course can be seen as a terrace in the fields, cutting across the angle on the west.

Salt routes – Salt was one of the most important commodities carried regularly over the moors to the medieval and early-modern

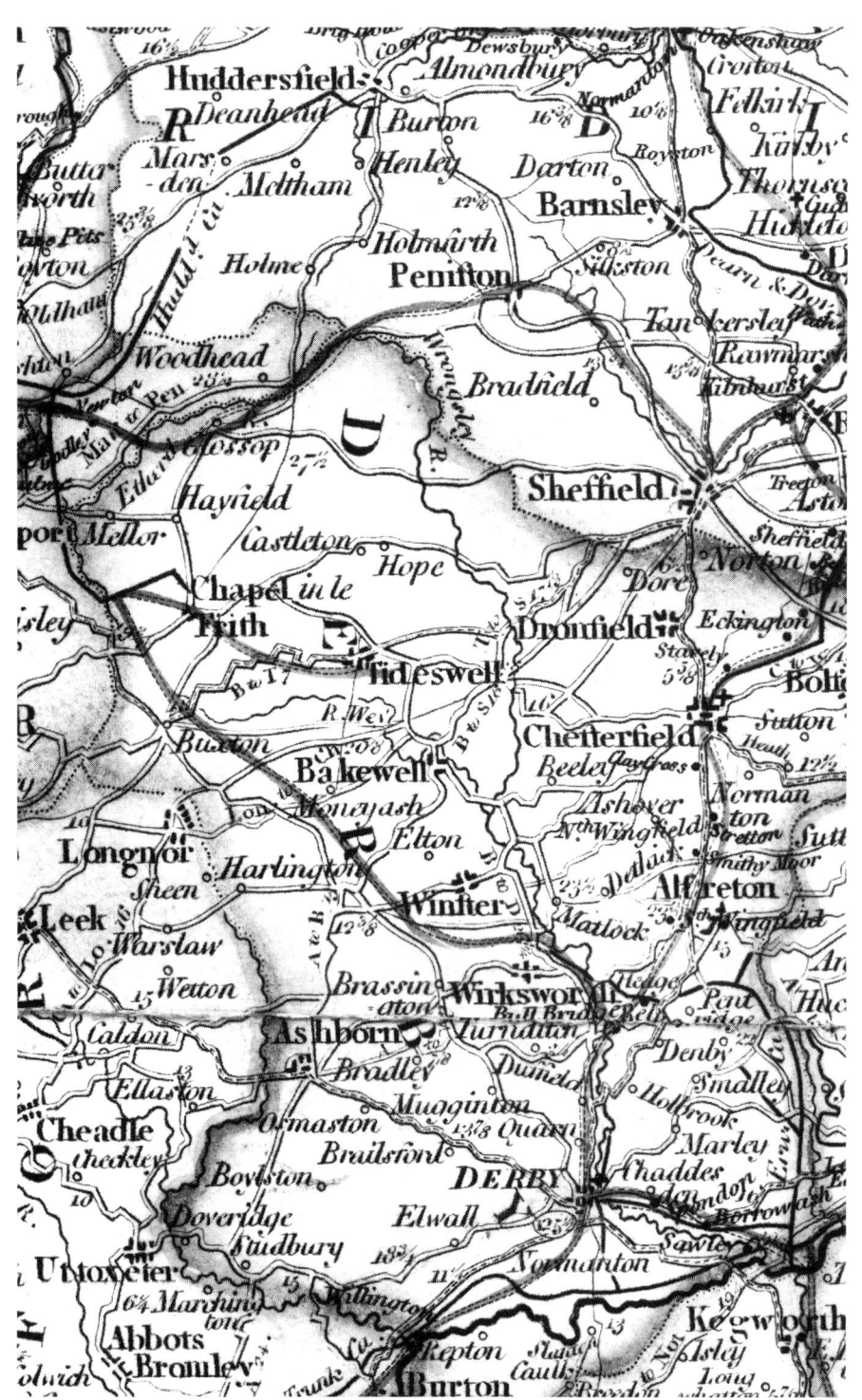

Part of J. Wyld's map of Britain 1843 (enlarged)

market towns of Yorkshire, Derbyshire and Nottinghamshire. It was essential for preserving food and adding flavour. In the days before refrigeration the people of the midland counties were able to get their supplies from the Cheshire *wiches* – Northwich, Middlewich and Nantwich. Distinctive names were given to the routes radiating from the wiches such as Saltersway, Salter Hill and Salter Ford. As the Derbyshire hills were often too steep and rough for carts, salt was mostly transported by packhorse.

With the aid of a map it is possible to trace part of an old salt route via Hartington (130604) to Chesterfield. Today the route is marked by a cart road (155594) and then a footpath south-eastwards to Upperhouse Farm (182592). From here there are three and a half miles of modern roads to Winster (240605). From Winster the salters could have gone to Chesterfield or Mansfield.

Turnpike roads – In the 1750's, 22 Acts of Parliament were passed for turnpike roads in Derbyshire, due in part to the increased traffic in minerals, particularly lead and iron. The industrialisation of Staffordshire and Derbyshire greatly influenced the rate of transport development and this area enjoyed one of the most comprehensive networks of turnpikes in the 18th and 19th centuries.

As early as 1725 an Act had been passed to improve the rough and narrow road from Buxton through Chapel-en-le-Frith to Manchester. This was the first turnpike road in the Peaks, and is now the main

Part of David & Charles 1st Edition OS Map, Sheet No 27

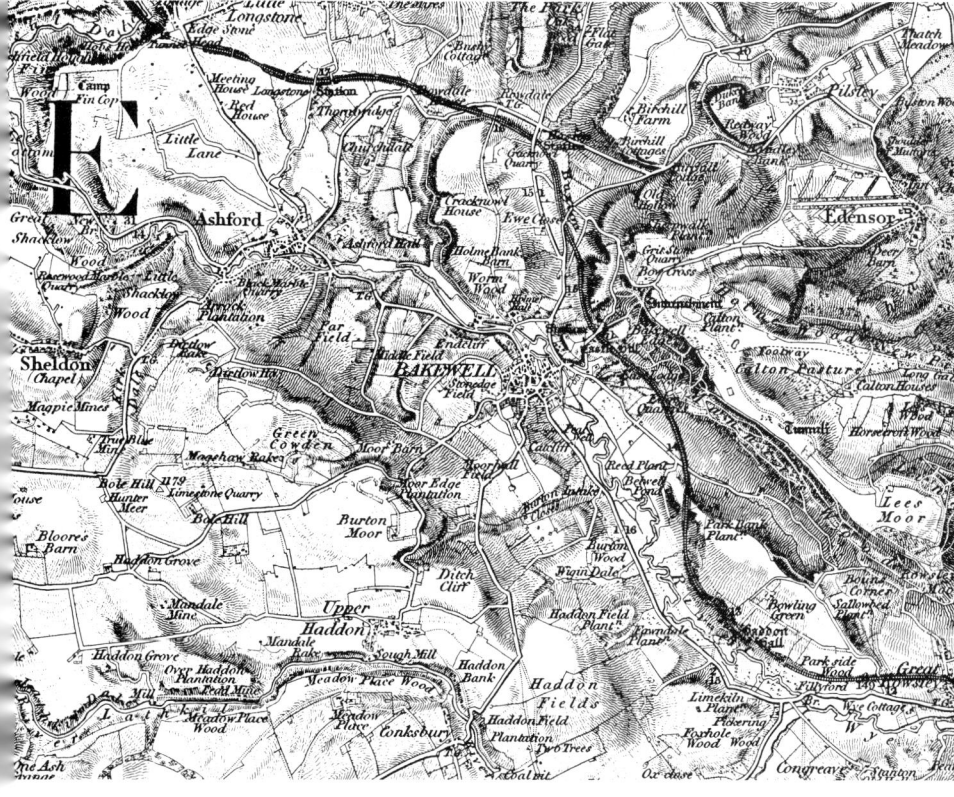

Manchester road, the A6. The rest of the A6 north from Derby developed in a piecemeal fashion, not being completed until 1818 when a narrow passageway was blasted through the solid limestone rock at Scathin Nick (296570), opening up a new approach to the Matlock gorge from the south.

Many stretches of turnpike road are still in use, though often as minor roads, and a few travellers' inns have also survived. One obvious example is the isolated Newhaven Hotel (167603) on the A515. It was built in 1800 by the fifth Duke of Devonshire with stabling for a hundred horses. An interesting story is told about the Hotel. According to J. B. Firth it was placed above the licensing laws by George IV who granted the Duke a 'free and perpetual licence' in return for a pleasant evening's entertainment. Unfortunately it now conforms to modern licensing hours!

Dovedale – symbol of Peakland beauty – Between its

A short tunnel through the rock on the High Peak trail (Picture: A. Burton)

8

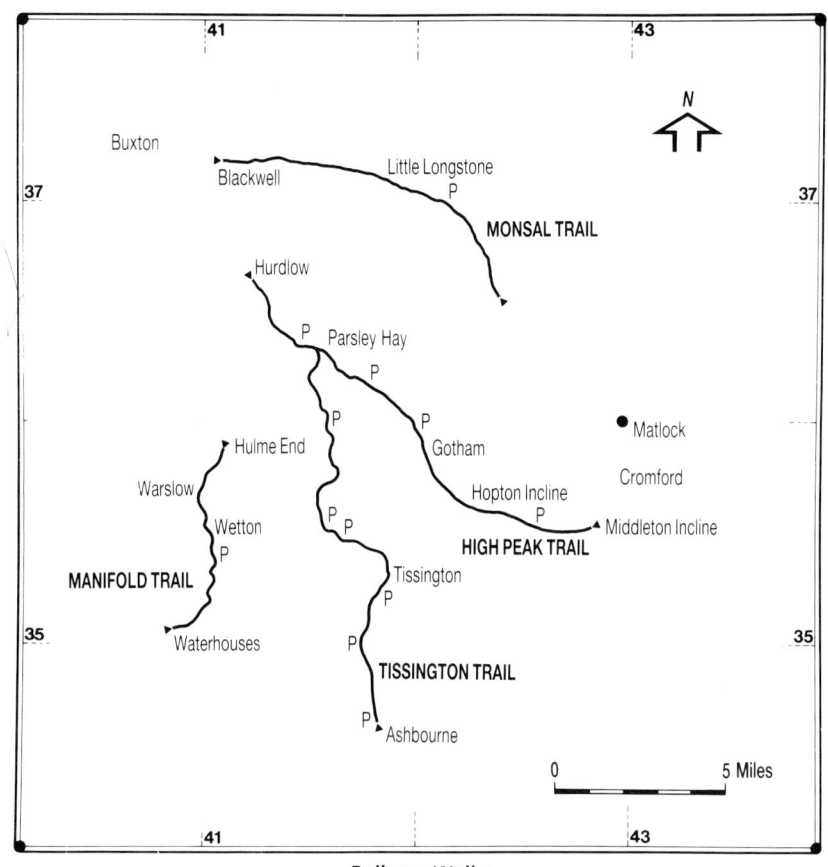

Railway Walks

source on Axe Edge (039685) and the village of Hollinsclough (063669) the Dove is pretty but unremarkable. But between here and Earl Sterndale are two extraordinary conical hills dominating the left bank, Chrome (070672) and Parkhouse (080670). One is lost for words at Beresford Dale and the limestone rocks (130585). The walk through Wolfscote Dale, Mill Dale and into Dove Dale proper is sheer beauty. Dovedale itself is a narrow ravine, its massive sides weathered into fantastic shapes. However, care should be taken when wandering over Ilam Rock (140531), Jacob's Ladder (144522), and the Twelve Apostles (144517). The weather can be both fickle and cruel. But for many the views along the River Dove are among the most cherished of the beautiful and fascinating Peaks.

Another fascinating walk is from Arbor Low (165637) to the Bull Ring. The first part of the walk is along the footpath to Monyash (152662) which runs on a north-westerly alignment to the disused mines and Ferndale. The route then continues the old industrial theme by following the lane past more disused lead mines and Knotlow (141677) to the villages of Flagg and Townhead (129691).

This part of the walk shows an interesting contrast in Peak District life. For although the area had its own lead-mining industry, and the villages, although small, were quite close together, the mining was always carried out in an essentially wild and rural setting.

9

TOWNS AND VILLAGES

Buxton (0573) in the River Wye valley was a substantial Roman settlement named *Aquae Arnemetiae* meaning 'The Spa of the Goddess of the Grove'. It is on the Roman road from Lincoln to Manchester at the site of 28° C hot water springs called the Well of St Ann (Patron Saint of Cripples), now beneath the modern Crescent. Following the withdrawal of the Romans, the settlement became a market town, which at 300m, is the highest in England, centred on the angular old market place with St Ann's Church and small 17th century houses. A steady tide of pilgrims patronised the Chapel of St Ann and took the 'cure' but this practice was prohibited by Henry VIII although the ban was rescinded during Elizabeth's reign. The establishment of the Spa came from successive Dukes of Devonshire, who were also lords of the manor. The first Duke, one century after pilgrimages had been reauthorised, built a bathhouse on the original site in 1710, but substantial growth of both facilities and patronage only came following the efforts of the 5th Duke to build the Crescent in 1784 and to provide baths, hotels and other facilities. In 1790, on the opposite side of the road, the magnificent Great Stables were built to accommodate horses and grooms with a central exercise area but in 1859 this was converted to the Devonshire Royal Hospital. A new church was built in 1811. Landscaping of the valley and slopes has added to the Spa's charm and given the opportunity to provide further facilities including the Palace Hotel in 1868 and the Opera House of 1905, which accommodates the annual Buxton Festival of Music and Arts which is internationally famed.

Chesterfield (3871), on the River Rother, was an Iron Age settlement and later the site of a Roman fort subsequently named Cestrefeld by the Anglo-Saxons. Mentioned in the Domesday Book, it became an agricultural centre with markets from 1165 and was given a charter by King John in 1204 making the town a 'free' borough and licensing markets and an annual fair. The building of the North Midland Railway in 1841 had brought George Stephenson to the town, where he continued to live until 1848. He was buried in Holy Trinity Church. The railway brought new industry including glass and pottery manufacture.

The Royal Oak, like the Peacock Heritage Centre, is a timber framed building from 1500. The latter is thought to have been a craftsman's guild and is now used commercially. An old inn, the Cock and Pynot (magpie), is now Revolution House following its use in 1688 by the Earls of Devonshire and Danby and Mr John D'Arcy in initiating the overthrow of James II (King 1685–88) and issuing the invitation for William of Orange to come to England.

Bakewell (2168), on both sides of the valley of the River Wye, has 15°C warm water springs signified in the town's Saxon name, and has been the site of settlements for many centuries. The church site has evidence of ancient use signifying a considerable following.

Ilam from Blore Pastures (Ref: 1349. Picture: D. Pratt)

In 1697 the Duke of Rutland built a bath house, in Bath Street, in which the bath is 10 × 5m and this may be viewed.

Significant expansion in the town, however, only followed after 1800 when a later Duke of Rutland aimed to create a spa comparable to that at Buxton. He realigned the streets and formed Rutland Square, replaced the timber buildings and built the Rutland Arms and the Stables. The bank followed in 1838. Other stone buildings were sited elsewhere in the town but the anticipated success never came, though the buildings remain.

Edensor (2569) is a model village developed from 1838–42 by the Duke of Devonshire and designed by his gardener Joseph Paxton, who also designed the Crystal Palace. The variety of architectural styles in the village is of interest.

Eyam (2176) has been the site of a church since Anglo-Saxon times. It was stricken by the plague in 1665 during which most of the inhabitants died. There is an annual commemoration service each August.

Matlock (3059) was known to the Romans who mined lead here at Rutland and Masson caverns high above the valley at Abraham Heights, named in more recent times by a local man who had scaled the Heights in Quebec with General Wolfe. Matlock is a series of villages along the scenic valley of the River Derwent, from south to north consisting of Matlock Bath, Old Matlock with St Giles Church, Matlock Green including

Knowleston Place and The Green, Matlock Dale and Matlock Bridge with the railway terminus. It also has a 15th century stone, four-arched bridge over the river leading to Matlock Bank. Thermal spring water was used medicinally at Matlock Bath in 1698 when a lead-lined wooden bath was installed but was replaced in 1725 by a substantial stone Bath House; hotels were constructed to accommodate visitors. In 1850 Mr John Smedley, a local textile manufacturer, developed Matlock Bank into a fashionable Spa, building Smedley's Hydro, a hydropathic centre with exercise areas and chapel, which provided treatments until 1955 when it was converted for use by the local council. The tram depot in Rutland Street operated tramcars with the steepest gradient track of any cable tramway. The valley is described as having a 'thousand views' and visitors can flock to Matlock to experience the many amenities which have replaced hydropathic cures.

Alton Towers (0743) in the River Churnet valley, was built from 1810 to 1852 by the Earls of Shrewsbury, with a compulsion to create something of unusual grandeur. It has pavilions, gables, towers and turrets but was used in World War II for troop training followed by several years' neglect which made it uninhabitable and beyond reasonable restoration. The grounds have been developed into a gigantic scenic playground.

Farm work before the tractor

PLACE NAMES

English place-names exist in layers, each associated with a stage in the development of English history.

The earliest layer of names on English maps dates from the arrival of the Celts about three thousand years ago. These names are more common in the North and West. Then, after the Roman occupation, it was the coming of the Angles and Saxons (5th to 7th centuries) which provided the chief source of place-names. Finally a layer of Scandinavian names was given to parts of North and East England by the Danish conquests (9th century) and the raids of the Norsemen (10th century).

Buxton (060730) is the 'bowing stone' or 'rocking stone'. *Matlock* (300600) is the 'moot oak'. The *Dove* is the 'dark river'.

Alton (070420) is the 'old farm', *Duffield* (340430) is the 'open space frequented by doves' and *Belper* (350470) is the 'beautiful retreat'. *Wirksworth* (285540) is 'Weorc's worth'; *worth* is Old English for 'enclosure'.

Between Uttoxeter and Etruria (Picture: D. Pratt)

Heage Windmill (Ref: 3650. Picture: A. Kind)

Chesterfield (380710) is the 'open space by the Roman station', *Apperknowle* (380780) is the 'apple-tree hill', *Totley* (310800) is the 'clearing of Tota's people' and *Bakewell* (220690) is 'Badeca's spring'. *Hucklow* (178778) is 'Hucca's hill', *Youlgreave* (208642) is the 'yellow grove', *Winster* (240605) is 'Wine's thorn-bush' and *Ripley* (400500) is the 'strip-shaped clearing'.

The study of the translations of English place-names, such as those above, will yield distinctive patterns to the perceptive observer. However care is required. Over the centuries many names which were originally the same have become distinct from each other. Conversely some names which are identical in their modern forms have evolved from different beginnings. Careful detective work is required to establish true origins but the hunt is a fascinating one.

Cromford (293565) is the 'ford at a bend in the river', *Crich* (350540) is 'hill' in the pre-English Britonic language, *Ashbourne* (180465) is the 'stream where ash-trees grow' and *Tissington* (175523) is the 'manor of Tidsige's people'. *Cheadle* (010430) is the 'wood', *Bradbourne* (210526) is the 'broad stream' and *Calver* (240747) is the 'slope where the calves graze', *Dronfield* (350780) is the 'open land infested by drones' and *Hopton* (258532) is the 'farm in the upland blind valley'. *Brassington* (230543) is the 'farm by the steep slope' and *Carsington* (250535) is the 'farm where the cress grows'.

CANALS AND RIVERS

The rivers that appear on this map are among the most beautiful in the country, with the valley of the Dove ranking as one of the most popular tourist attractions in the region, but they have never been important as trading routes. Water transport came into prominence with the canal age.

The first canal to be built was the Chesterfield, which was begun under the direction of James Brindley in 1771, but not completed until after his death. It opened in 1777 and was successful in part. The Chesterfield end had many locks, which made it an inconvenient canal to use, but more important was subsidence caused by mining which caused a tunnel to collapse. By 1896, the Chesterfield end was closed. Now, however, work has begun on re-opening this very attractive waterway, which runs into Chesterfield from 400747. The towpath can still be walked.

The Caldon Canal is a near contemporary of the Chesterfield. It was completed in 1779, and it too became derelict, but restoration is now complete. It is one of the most beautiful of the country's canals, particularly the section along the Churnet Valley shown here. It is a narrow, twisting route which ends in a short tunnel. Theoretically, this is navigable, but it is low and narrow and it is a lucky cruiser that emerges with its paintwork intact. Beyond it is the terminus of Froghall Wharf. This is a fascinating area of old limekilns and the remains of the tramway system that brought stone from the quarries at Caldon Low (0749) which gave the canal its name. There are horsedrawn boat trips from Froghall.

The third canal, the Cromford, completes a trio that share a history of decay and restoration. It originally ran from Cromford to connect with the Erewash, but like the Chesterfield, mining subsidence caused a tunnel collapse which has never been repaired. Nevertheless, the section shown on this map is full of interest. At Cromford Wharf (300570) the old buildings are now home to a steam museum owned by the Cromford Canal Society, and from here there are passenger trips in a horsedrawn boat. The canal runs past the end of the Cromford and High Peak Railway to Leawood pumping station, which lifted water from the Derwent to supply the canal. The

Navigable Waterways

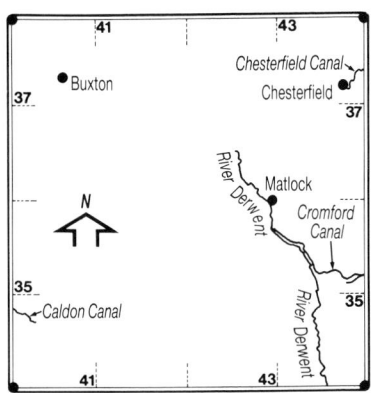

1849 beam engine has been restored and is regularly steamed. The canal then crosses the Derwent on a high stone aqueduct and continues down the valley to Bullbridge, where another stopped tunnel (350519) brings proceedings to a close. Originally, the line continued east past the canal reservoir at 400518.

There are a number of reservoirs in the area, offering facilities to the public. Ogston (3760) has a picnic area, club sailing and game fishing; Linacre (3272) has game fishing, a nature reserve and walks and trails. Lightwood (0575), Barbrook (2777) and Crowhole (3174) have nature reserves. Errwood (0175) has trout fishing, sailing and sailboarding and Fernilee (0177) has good birdwatching.

> David & Charles produce a wide ranging list of books covering every aspect of the British countryside. The full catalogue is £1 but write to us at Brunel House, Newton Abbot, Devon TQ12 4PU and we will send you a copy with our compliments.

The canal wharf, Froghall (Ref: 0247. Picture: D. Pratt)

CASTLES, CHURCHES, HALLS

Eyam (2176) Church of St Lawrence, despite extensive restoration in the 19th century, is a pleasant mixture of an Early English (13th century) chancel, a Perpendicular (1330–1530) tower and the antiquity of a Norman font. Between the clerestory windows are rare 16th century paintings of the 12 tribes of Israel. The greatest delight, however, is afforded by the 8th century Saxon cross in the churchyard. Such crosses, even if fragmented, are rare but this one has the distinction of having a shaft complete with head and arms and all with choice, inscribed spiral and other patterns. The sundial over the church door is inscribed so that one can calculate both local and international time. Eyam Hall is a 'dwelling house with outbuildings' built in 1676, ten years after the arrival of the appalling plague. It is stone built and has gables and mullioned windows.

Wirksworth (2853) Church of St Mary is ambitiously large and has a chancel with aisles, a crossing steeple and nave. It dates from 1272 but with 19th century restoration. In Anglo-Saxon times Wirksworth had an association with Repton and it is likely that there was some ecclesiastic building here, possibly a chapel. In 1820 an Anglo-Saxon coffin lid was discovered, dated about 800, which now rests near the north wall. It is richly decorated with stories from the life of Christ. In walls of the north and south transepts and north aisle there are Norman architectural fragments. One of the fonts is Norman. There is an ala-baster slab to Ralph Gell who died in 1564, sculptured by Royleys at Burton-on-Trent. This firm was active at that time with alabaster work and their other examples should be sought.

Hognaston (2350) Church of St Batholomew has a Norman doorway with a tympanum having an incised picture of a bishop and animals. The tower is 13th century and the chancel 14th century but with rebuilding in the 19th century. The font is also Norman.

Tissington (1752) Church of St Mary has a broad, square Norman tower, Norman south doorway with tympanum and a Norman font with incised patterns of animals. The remainder was made to look like Norman work but rebuilt in the 19th century. Tissington Hall is Jacobean with a plain facade having mullioned and transomed win-

The Bonsall Cross (Ref: 2758)

The Baptist Chapel, Crich (Ref: 350541. Picture: A. Kind)

dows. The village is noted for its annual thanksgiving and well dressing and is thought to have originated the annual ceremony celebrated on Ascension Day both here and also in other villages.

Ashover (3463) Church of All Saints was built from the 13–15th century and is low, embattled and steepled. The Norman font of 1200 is made of lead, which is appropriate for a lead mining area, and is decorated with standing, human figures framed in arcading with upper and lower friezes. The cracked bell, still in use, is reputed to have cracked whilst being rung, perhaps overzealously, to herald the news of the defeat of Napoleon in 1815.

Youlgrave (2164) Church of All Saints has a Norman south arcade and west end of the nave. Other parts of the nave are from a little later and the tower is 15th century. The stone font is Norman, standing on short columns and with a small, additional receptacle at the side called a stoup and decorated with animal and leaf patterns. It was 'brought' from Elton (2261) in 1838 and they now use a replica.

Cromford (2957) is the town of Richard Arkwright (1732–92). He built Willersley Castle (2957) in 1689–90, complete with turrets and battlements, in which he planned to live but, because of a fire in 1791, he died before being able to do so. It commands superb views of the valley and is now used as a Methodist Rest Home. He built the Church of Cromford St Mary from

1792 and it still has the original small west tower, now with an added open porch. There was extensive reconstruction in 1858. There are monuments to Mrs Arkwright (1820) and Charles Arkwright (1850). The Sir Richard Arkwright & Co, Cromford Mill of 1771, next to the church, was the first cotton-spinning mill to be operated by water-power and heralded industrial mechanisation. Across the 15th century bridge spanning the River Derwent is North Street, where he built houses for workers from 1771–6, an infrequent social benefaction at that time. Along the B5023 road southwards there is the tall chimney of a pumping engine used for lifting water to convey it across the valley to the mill and canal and built by Arkwright and his consortium. Here was an ingenious man with the vision and courage to introduce his inventions.

Chesterfield (3871) Church of St Mary and All Saints is famed for its crooked spire which may have been caused by differential warping of the timbers by there being more heat from the sun on the south sides than the north sides. In addition to the crossing tower there is an aisled nave and a chancel. There are many side chapels and these reflect the wealth of the benefactors. Parts of the church date from 1234 and there was substantial 19th century restoration. The nave arcades, chancel arch, and the rood screen (of 1915) beneath the latter, are impressive. The stone font is Norman and has decorations of

Alton Castle (Ref: 0742. Picture: D. Pratt)

leaves and a cross. The Church of the Annunciation (RC) was built in 1854, to a design by J. Hansom, with a large broad tower of 1874. The Unitarian Elder Yard Chapel was built in 1697.

Chatsworth House (2670) set in 1,500 acres of parkland, should be approached from the south to afford good distant views as one approaches. The estate was bought in 1549 by Bess of Hardwick and her second husband, Sir William Cavendish. Succeeding Dukes of Devonshire have continued to embellish the property. The rooms display many beautiful examples of art and craftsmanship. Altogether, visiting Chatsworth is a unique experience. They demolished the existing house at Chatsworth and erected another from 1551 and their Hunting Tower, sited in the woods above, still survives.

Ilam Hall gateway (Ref: 1350. Picture: D. Pratt)

Leawood Pumphouse on the Cromford Canal (Ref: 3155. Picture: A. Kind)

RAILWAYS

This map shows part of a busy main line system with its branch lines, and a great many derelict railways which have found a new use as footpaths and cycleways. The latter offer so much of interest – and not just to railway enthusiasts – that the emphasis will be placed on them. But first, the active lines can be briefly summarised.

The North Midland Railway was authorised in 1836, with George Stephenson as the engineer. It was to be part of a grand scheme to link York and Leeds to London and it succeeded, but Stephenson was a great believer in easy gradients and he did not like the look of the hilly country between Chesterfield and Sheffield so he took a wide detour to the east, curving round to Rotherham. This is the line from 362400 to 400749. The citizens of Sheffield were not, however, content with branch line status and the direct route – the present main line – was soon built, leaving the map via the sort of heavy engineering works that Stephenson had avoided, the tunnel at 338800. The whole system was incorporated into the Midland Railway, which opened a branch to Ripley in 1856, leaving the map at 400485.

The disused line leaving the map at 400519 from Ambergate is the grandly named Ambergate, Nottingham, Boston and Eastern Junction Railway, also destined to be swallowed by the Midland. Chesterfield got an extra line, joining it to the Great Central, further east via a loop, opened in 1893, leaving the map as a disused line at 400703. Chesterfield also had a direct route to Lincoln, part of a grander scheme that was never completed.

The freight line to Wirksworth was a Midland branch, leaving the main line at Duffield (345435). What appears to be a branch line to Matlock was in fact part of a much grander scheme, the Manchester, Buxton, Matlock and Midlands Junction Railway. This began in optimism in 1846, but floundered for lack of cash and Ambergate (349516) to Buxton was not open until 1863. A separate company, the Stockport, Disley and Whaley Bridge Railway, completed the still operative line north of Buxton. It opened on the same day, and leaves the map at 023800. Unfortunately, the former line was now Midland and the latter London and North Western Railway, and the two failed to agree, so the

Old railway line on the Tissington trail (Picture: A. Burton)

22

Midland made another connection, via the line leaving the map at 053800.

The line between Buxton and Bakewell was not universally welcomed. John Ruskin spoke of the old valley as home of the gods, and cursed the railway builders. 'The valley is gone, and the Gods with it; and now, every fool in Buxton can be at Bakewell in half-an-hour; and every fool in Bakewell at Buxton; which you think a lucrative process of exchange – you Fools Everywhere.' Ruskin would no doubt be happy to know that the trains have gone, the beauty and peace are restored – and he might even acknowledge that the old line, now the Monsal Trail, has added something to the scene. The walk begins at Bakewell, where the line heads north before swinging east to join the Wye Valley, which provided the engines with the only feasible route through the hills. There is a short tunnel, before the old line emerges to cross the Wye, not for the last time, in a high viaduct. Monsal Head viaduct

Middleton Top Engine House (Ref: 275552. Picture: A. Burton)

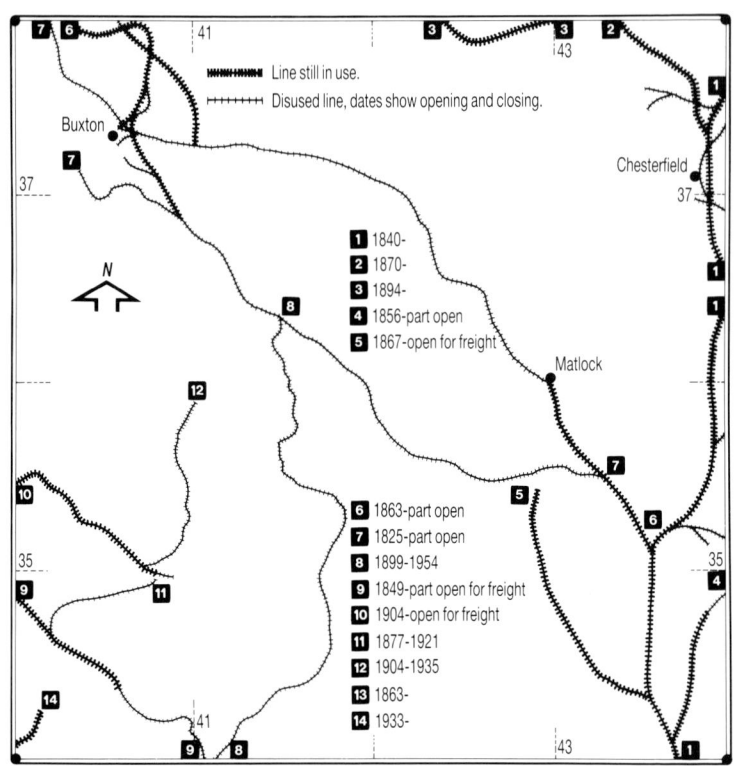

The railway network, past and present

(183715) may not be the mightiest in the railway system, but few have a more beautiful setting. After this, the engineers had to work hard to keep their line on a reasonable route. It clings to the hillside on a narrow ledge, cuts through in short tunnels, and is forced into two more river crossings in Miller's Dale, one on an iron and one on a stone viaduct. These airy passages help to make this a most spectacular walk through some of the loveliest of Peak District countryside. The trail ends at 113726. The length of line south of Matlock has its own pleasures for rail travellers, including an extraordinary station at Cromford (303574) like a miniature French chateau, with an equally grand villa for the station master to complement it.

There is a possibility that trains may one day steam again between Buxton and Matlock. A modest start has been made with the establishment of the Peak Rail Steam Centre at Buxton Midland Station (060738). There is a collection of locomotives and rolling stock, but at the present only a few hundred metres of track.

The Monsal Trail is only one of four long distance railway walks shown on this map. The first follows the line of the earliest railway shown on this map, the Cromford and High Peak. This was built originally in 1825 as a tramway, intended for use not by steam locomotives, but by horses, and it was to link two canals, the Cromford in the east, the Peak Forest in the west, via a line across the hills. The rails were mounted on stone blocks, leaving the centre of the

24

track clear for the horses, and the hills were overcome by a series of inclines, up which the trains were hauled by stationary steam engines at the tops of the slopes. The route can be traced from the old transit warehouse at 314557, where goods were exchanged between canal and railway. It follows the line of the canal to the old maintenance shed, now a museum telling the whole story of the railway from its horse-drawn up to its later steam days.

Then the climb begins up the inclines: even when a passenger service was introduced on the line, and locomotives were used, the passengers still had to get out and walk – which explains why the 1874 timetable shows a journey time of 3 hours 25 minutes for the 30 mile distance. The effort of climbing the inclines is well worthwhile for it brings one out to Middleton Top Engine House (275552) which still has its old steam engine, now fully restored and demonstrations are given using compressed air. Those

A bridge on the disused branch railway at Bullbridge (Ref: 358522. Picture: A. D. Kind)

whose legs are tired can hire cycles here, and they are also available at Parsley Hay (148638). The railway now threads its way through typical Derbyshire limestone scenery, of hill farms and fields marked by dry stone walls that straggle out across the hillside. There is one more incline at Hopton (2554) which begins gently at 1 in 60 but rises to a fierce 1 in 14 at the top – yet it was worked by conventional locomotives. Having reached its summit, the old line twists and turns to stay there. It reaches a slightly disappointing conclusion, stopped by quarry workings at 1067.

At Parsley Hay, there is a junction with the line that ran down to Ashbourne, where it met the North Staffordshire Railway, the latter line having opened in 1852. This extension, opened in 1899, is now another walk and cycleway, the Tissington Trail. It is a route that falls steeply all the way to Ashbourne, for nearly 200 metres, and which cuts its way ruthlessly through the hills. Immediately after leaving the High Peak Trail the Tissington disappears into a deep, rocky cutting, before setting off in a great S-bend round the hills. The car park at 1561 has one of the rare survivors of the railway past, the old Hartington signal box. Throughout its course this line is forced into severe gradients and extravagant curves to cope with the hilly landscape. One wonders if it was all worthwhile for the line had scarcely celebrated its 50th birthday before it was closed: but it does make a fine trail.

It was at least more successful than the next line to be turned into a path. The Leek and Manifold Light Railway was opened in 1904. It ran from the Froghall to Caldon tramway opened in 1777, but the North Staffordshire Railway had to build extensions from their main line, which can be seen going down the Churnet Valley from 000491 to 103400. The Leek and Manifold was a narrow gauge line, which managed to fit in seven halts on the 13km journey to Hulme End, a terminus of no greater significance than any of the halts. It was supposed to bring in flocks of tourists: they never arrived and the line closed in 1935 and was at once converted into a footpath and bridleway. It is easy to see why the promoter saw it as a tourist route, for the Manifold valley with its soaring limestone crags is almost as picturesque as neighbouring Dovedale, and contains the spectacular Thor's Cave. The end is a little sad: the muddle of wooden buildings by the road (103595) are all that remain of the headquarters of the old railway.

Fish-bellied rail on stone sleeper blocks

If you live in England or Wales David & Charles have reproduced a Victorian Ordnance survey map of your area which is available for only £3.50 post and packing inclusive. You can buy it from your bookshop or write to us at Brunel House, Newton Abbot, Devon TQ12 4PU.

ANCIENT SITES

The most spectacular ancient site is also the oldest known inhabited site in the region. Thor's Cave (098549) is a great, natural opening in the cliffs above the Manifold valley, which is known to have been occupied in the Old Stone Age or Paleolithic period, around 10,000 years ago. Evidence of occupation is even stronger for what is, in archaeological terms, the comparatively recent past of around 200 BC.

The New Stone or Neolithic Age is characterised by two types of remains: the henges and burial chambers. Henges must certainly have had ritual significance, but what form it took has long since been forgotten. At its simplest a henge consists of a circular or oval ditch and bank, though it may also be associated with standing stones. Arbor Low (160636) is a classic henge, with an oval bank 83 metres by 76 metres, inside which is a ring of limestone blocks, once presumably upright but now fallen. Later Bronze Age burial mounds were made by the ring, making this an exceptionally fine site in a splendid open position. Bull Ring Henge (078783) must once have looked very similar, but quarrying has resulted in the disappearance of the stones and the destruction of much of the earthworks. There are other stone circles on Stanton Moor. The best preserved is the Nine Ladies (249633), a ring of boulders in a low, rubble wall, enclosed by a somewhat superfluous modern wall. The area also has dozens of small cairns, excavation of which has revealed cremations and a rich array of grave goods from the Bronze Age. The Nine Ladies are, almost inevitably, said to have been women punished for dancing on the Sabbath.

The most common form of Neolithic burial is the long barrow, generally a massive oblong mound, such as the Ringham barrow (169664), but cairns were also constructed. These were carefully built up from stones, and then covered over. Examples are Five Wells (124711), Green Low (233580), Minninglow (209573) and Long Low (122539). The latter consists of two mounds, joined by a bank, on which it is said fairies dance on Christmas Eve. Not all stone circles are Neolithic. Nine Stones Close (227627) dates from the later Bronze Age, and has not nine but four stones – though there were once more. Legend, once again, has them as ladies who dance, this time at midnight.

The old, green road above Monsal Dale (Ref: 171717)

27

Bronze Age burials were traditionally under round barrows, and there are some impressive examples: End Low (156606), Elam (136527) and Hob Hurst's House (287692), named after the supernatural being, Hobthrush.

The one Iron Age site – though the actual date has not been confirmed – is Castle Naze (054784). The fort consists of a promontory where the steep sides and crags afford natural protection. The neck is closed off by walls and a ditch.

The David & Charles Britain series is an exciting range of books covering, The Lake District, The Peak District, The Northumbrian Uplands, The Pembrokeshire Coast National Park, and Snowdonia. There are several others planned.

Each volume – written out of deep personal knowledge of the area – provides a thorough background and guide to archaeology, natural history, the development of the landscape, and architectural styles. Each book is at least 200 pages, hardback and illustrated in colour. Buy them from your bookshop or write to us at Brunel House, Newton Abbot, Devon TQ12 4PU.

The henge monument at Arbor Low
(Ref: 1663. Picture: Cambridge University Collection of Air Photographs)

NATURE

The southern half of the Peak District National Park, known as the White Peak, is a plateau of carboniferous limestone, dissected by the Derbyshire Dales. Several of these form the Derbyshire Dales National Nature Reserve: Lathkill Dale (190658) is one, with a river which partly stops flowing in dry weather. The upper section has some imposing limestone crags, and the Dale is particularly interesting for its plants. The original woodland cover of ash, has been modified by planted Scots pine, beech and sycamore. Lower down the valley, the ash is joined by rowan, wych elm, guelder rose and the rare rock whitebeam. Lily-of-the-Valley, mezereon, water avens, bird's-nest orchid and green helleborine are found on the woodland floor. Other parts of the Dale are grassland with much false oat-grass and typical limestone plants including bird's-foot trefoil, thyme, marjoram and rock-rose. Lead mining spoil tips are covered by common spotted orchids.

Other Dales worth visiting are Monks Dale (135743) with woodland, grassland and wet flushes; Cressbrook Dale (173739), where scrub invading the grassland is dominated by aspen; Monsal Dale (183715); and, of course, the very popular Dovedale (144525), where the oak and lime trees are usually found together, and the scrub includes a substantial growth of holly.

The Manifold (100543) and Hamp valleys are less well-known to tourists, but boast dramatic limestone scenery, rich in limestone plants: salad burnet, eyebright, harebell, marjoram, rock-rose, common spotted and greater butterfly orchids in ash woodlands and wildflower meadows. Whinchat and linnet live in the hawthorn scrub on the higher slopes.

Two small Derbyshire Wildlife Trust reserves are linked by a footpath: Parsley Hay (147628), a limestone cutting in what is now the Tissington Trail, following a disused railway line, has heather and cowslips and attracts many birds and insects; at the other end of the Tissington Trail, Tissington Station Cutting (which may be overlooked from 182525) is ash

The Lily-of-the-Valley, which is commonly known as a garden plant, actually grows wild in dry woodlands, where it spreads readily by underground rhizomes. The sprays of delicate, white, bell-like flowers emit a heady perfume in May and June, turning to red berries later in the summer

The mill weirs at Belper on the River Derwent (Ref: 345482. Picture: A. Kind)

woodland with grassland and marsh.

In the north the National Trust's Longshaw Estates (260790) demonstrate the other rock of the Peak District, millstone grit. Fine parkland, moorland and wooded streams attract many species of birds, and there are several nature walks through the area.

The wildlife interest of this area is by no means confined to the National Park. Buxton Country Park (050727) has a nature trail through its broadleaved woodland beside the spectacular Poole's Cavern. Coombes Valley (005530) and near-by Rough Knipe are both RSPB reserves in Staffordshire. The former is a wooded valley, with some old oak woodland, a small stream, and open grassland, offering a range of habitats to attract tits, redstarts, nuthatch and all three British woodpeckers. Grey wagtail, dipper, kingfisher and heron all inhabit the area of the stream, and badgers are also present. The smaller Rough Knipe reserve is also woodland and is noted for its pied flycatchers, sparrowhawks and redstarts.

A totally different Derbyshire nature reserve, well outside the National Park, is Cromford Canal, which in its derelict state is a haven for water plants such as bur-reed, bulrush, water forget-me-not, yellow flag and reed sweetgrass. The water is alive with animals – pond snails, water boatmen, pond skaters and water mites; dragonflies and damselflies are plentiful in summer. Butterflies abound. Birds include moorhen, coot and heron.

INDUSTRIAL ARCHAEOLOGY

The village of Cromford is a place of worldwide significance in the history of industry. It was here in 1771 that Richard Arkwright established the world's first cotton mill, in which the machinery was powered by water. It began the process by which textile production moved out of the home and into the factory: Cromford is the first mill town. The original mill, much altered, can still be seen (298569) and is currently being restored, but one can get a much clearer idea of what an early Arkwright mill was like from the mill he opened nearby in 1783. Masson Mill (294573) has been extended, but the old part with its cupola and distinctive Venetian windows is still very clear. Equally impressive is the massive weir across the river that diverted water to a leat which carried it away to the water wheels. But Cromford represented a social as well as an industrial change. A new town had to be built for the mill workers, and very fine it was too: far better than the slums that developed in later cotton towns. The best examples can be seen in Cromford's North Street, terraces of sturdy 3-storeyed stone houses. The upper floors have the traditional, long 'weavers' windows', for at first only spinning was mechanised. The men worked up here at their looms, while the women and children went to the mill. It is interesting to compare North Street with the house Arkwright built for himself out of the profits, Willersley Castle (296573).

Arkwright's partner, who helped finance him, was a local hosiery manufacturer, Jebediah Strutt, who also built mills. A complex of mills grew up beside the weirs on the Derwent at Belper (345480). The 1804 North Mill is dwarfed by its larger neighbours. Arkwright expanded into Lancashire, but the local spinners, fearing for their livelihood, burned down his mill and threatened to march on Derbyshire. The mill bridge still has its gun embrasures, cut to repel the rioters: they never came. Strutt, too, provided fine housing, notably in Long Row. These early mills were often handsome buildings, and one of the most impressive is Calver Mill, built in 1803 (245744). Cressbrook Mill (173728) was begun by Arkwright in 1779. Behind it, with Gothic gables, is the apprentice house, home to as many as 300 orphans or poor children, sent to work in the mill.

Lead mining in Derbyshire goes back at least as far as Roman times – and there is a carving of a medieval lead miner known as 'T'owd man' in Wirksworth church. Among the easily recognised early workings are the rakes, looking like natural chasms, as the miners dug their way down from the surface. There are a number to be seen on Longstone Moor (1973 to 2273). Later, deep mines became necessary. The surface remains can be very impressive, and the finest are those of Magpie Mine, Sheldon (173682), with its two engine houses, gunpowder store, shafts with headgear and a surviving jigger, a machine used to separate the ore from the rubble. The story of lead mining is told in detail at the Peak District Mining Museum in Matlock Bath (294583). As well as conventional displays, visitors have a chance to climb shafts and work pumps and special underground visits can also be arranged. Nearby, in Temple Road, the old Temple Mine is being developed to show mining techniques of the 1920s and '30s.

Quarrying is still an important industry in the area, and now a National Stone Centre has been established here (285555). Work began on this important project, which straddles the High Peak Trail, in 1988. The aim is to use the existing quarry sites to show all kinds of techniques and machinery in appropriate settings. There will be conventional exhibitions and a training centre. One use to which limestone has been put is the creation of lime, by burning it in kilns. Two big industrial limekilns have been preserved by the Monsal Trail (137734).

A quarry site that has been put to a very different use can be seen at Crich (347549), which is now

Crich Tramway Museum (Ref: 3452. Picture: Crich Tramway Museum)

*The remains of the Magpie Lead Mine
(Ref: 173682. Picture: Peak District Mining Museum)*

home to the National Tramway Museum. The visitors first meet the trams in the appropriate setting of an Edwardian street, fronted by the old Assembly Rooms from Derby. After seeing the trams on show, visitors can then spend as long as they like riding the trams on a splendid scenic route. This is a unique collection of trams from around the world, covering development right back to the Victorian age. Another slightly unlikely quarry survivor is the preserved quarry winding engine on the National Trust's Longshaw Estate (252789).

Caudwell Mill (255657) is a water powered grain mill, built in 1874. It is unlike most early mills in that instead of grindstones to crush the wheat to make flour, it uses rollers. The introduction of roller mills in the 1870s brought the closure of most of the small traditional wind and water mills in Britain. Caudwell Mill is itself quite small for a roller mill.

The Red House Stables at Darley Dale (277623) house a collection of horsedrawn vehicles and equipment. Local history is given a very up to date image in the Wirksworth Heritage Centre in Crown Yard, a former silk and velvet mill. Apart from seeing conventional displays, visitors can play a computer game to rescue an injured miner or visit an imitation cavern. Equally up to the minute is Buxton's Micrarium in The Crescent. Here one can use push button remote-controlled microscopes to explore the natural world. Finally, the Heights of Abraham at Matlock (296585) offer a mine, a cavern and a Victorian prospect tower, all reached by cable car.

TOURIST INFORMATION

Local Information Centres
East Midlands Tourist Board
Exchequergate
Lincoln LN2 1PZ
(0522) 531521
Contact EMTB to obtain their "Guide to the Shires of Middle England" for more details of accommodation and attractions.
Buxton
The Crescent
Derbyshire SK17 6BQ
(0298) 5106
Matlock Bath
The Pavilion
Derbyshire DE4 3NR
(0629) 55082
Chesterfield
Peacock Information and Heritage Centre, Low Pavement
Derbyshire S40 1PB
(0246) 207777
Bakewell
Old Market Hall, Bridge Street
Derbyshire DE4 1DS
(062 981) 3227
Ashbourne
13 Market Place
Derbyshire DE6 1EU
(0335) 43666
Automobile Association
Chesterfield Travel
56 Knifesmithgate, Chesterfield
Derbyshire S40 1RQ
(0246) 204777

Travel
RAC road information
Sheffield (0742) 737944
Rail information
Sheffield (0742) 726411
Bus information
Chesterfield (0246) 276666
Air information
Birmingham (021 767) 5511

Nature Reserves
The Royal Society for Nature Conservation (0522-752326) provides contacts for local Wildlife Trusts who can advise on the best nature reserves to visit.

Touring Companions want you to enjoy the countryside without any problems for you, other visitors, or the people who must live and work there all year round. Please remember that there is no general right to wander in the countryside, although trespass is seldom a criminal offence. Stay on the rights of way marked on the Ordnance Survey map unless there is clear indication that access is permitted, or you have asked permission. Remember that not all disused railway lines are open to the public. Always obey the Country Code.

Enjoy the countryside and respect its life and work.
Guard against all risk of fire.
Fasten all gates.
Keep your dogs under close control.
Keep to public paths across farmland.
Use gates and stiles to cross fences, hedges and walls.
Leave livestock, crops and machinery alone.
Take your litter home.
Help to keep all water clean.
Protect wildlife, plants and trees.
Take special care on country roads.
Make no unnecessary noise.

National Grid references reproduced by permission of the Ordnance Survey, Southampton.

Hartington Hall, Derbyshire (Picture: D. Widdicombe)
Bridge over the River Manifold at Ilam (Ref: 1350. Picture: D. Pratt)

Authors and artists in this volume include:

A. Burton, A. & A. Heaton, S. S. Kind, D. Young, E. Danielson,
S. Qureshi, J. Slocombe, R. Laight, A. Clift.